**This book is to be returned on or before
the last date stamped below.**

2 0 DEC 2003	0 9 MAY 2006	
1 3 MAY 2004		
1 8 AUG 2004	2 2 SEP 2007	
1 5 OCT 2004	- 4 JAN 2008	
1 8 JUN 2005	- 8 JUN 2010	
2 7 JUL 2005	2 9 JUN 2010	
2 5 NOV 2008		

**LEARNING FOR LIFE
LONDON BOROUGH OF SUTTON LIBRARIES**

RENEWALS   Please quote: date of return, your ticket number
                                 and computer label number for each item.

Francis Frith's

SURREY
LIVING MEMORIES

photographs of the mid twentieth century

Francis Frith's

SURREY
LIVING MEMORIES

Martin Andrew

FRITH
BOOK Co

First published in the United Kingdom in 2002 by
Frith Book Company Ltd

Hardback Edition 2002
ISBN 1-85937-328-3

British Library Cataloguing in Publication Data

Francis Frith's Surrey Living Memories
Martin Andrew

Frith Book Company Ltd
Frith's Barn, Teffont,
Salisbury, Wiltshire SP3 5QP
Tel: +44 (0) 1722 716 376
Email: info@francisfrith.co.uk
www.francisfrith.co.uk

Printed and bound in Great Britain

Front Cover: Surrey, Hindhead, the Corner Shop c1965 H86056

As with any historical database the Frith archive is constantly being corrected and improved
and the publishers would welcome information on omissions or inaccuracies

contents

Francis Frith: Victorian Pioneer

FRANCIS FRITH, Victorian founder of the world-famous photographic archive, was a complex and multi-talented man. A devout Quaker and a highly successful Victorian businessman, he was both philosophic by nature and pioneering in outlook.

By 1855 Francis Frith had already established a wholesale grocery business in Liverpool, and sold it for the astonishing sum of £200,000, which is the equivalent today of over £15,000,000. Now a multi-millionaire, he was able to indulge his passion for travel. As a child he had pored over travel books written by early explorers, and his fancy and imagination had been stirred by family holidays to the sublime mountain regions of Wales and Scotland. 'What a land of spirit-stirring and enriching scenes and places!' he had written. He was to return to these scenes of grandeur in later years to 'recapture the thousands of vivid and tender memories', but with a different purpose. Now in his thirties, and captivated by the new science of photography, Frith set out on a series of pioneering journeys to the Nile regions that occupied him from 1856 until 1860.

Intrigue and Adventure

He took with him on his travels a specially-designed wicker carriage that acted as both dark-room and sleeping chamber. These far-flung journeys were packed with intrigue and adventure. In his life story, written when he was sixty-three, Frith tells of being held captive by bandits, and of fighting 'an awful midnight battle to the very point of surrender with a deadly pack of hungry, wild dogs'. Sporting flowing Arab costume, Frith arrived at Akaba by camel seventy years before Lawrence, where he encountered 'desert princes and rival sheikhs, blazing with jewel-hilted swords'.

During these extraordinary adventures he was assiduously exploring the desert regions bordering the Nile and patiently recording the antiquities and peoples with his camera. He was the first photographer to venture beyond the sixth cataract. Africa was still the mysterious 'Dark Continent', and Stanley and Livingstone's historic meeting was a decade into the future. The conditions for picture taking confound belief. He laboured for hours in his wicker dark-room in the sweltering heat of the desert, while the volatile chemicals fizzed dangerously in their trays. Often he was forced to work in remote tombs and caves where conditions were cooler. Back in London he exhibited his photographs and was 'rapturously cheered' by members of the Royal Society. His reputation as a photographer was made overnight. An eminent modern historian has likened their impact on the population of the time to that on our own generation of the first photographs taken on the surface of the moon.

Venture of a Life-Time

Characteristically, Frith quickly spotted the opportunity to create a new business as a specialist publisher of photographs. He lived in an era of immense and sometimes violent change. For the poor in the early part of Victoria's reign work was a drudge and the hours long, and people had precious little free time to enjoy themselves. Most had no transport other than a cart or gig at their disposal, and had not travelled far beyond the boundaries of their own town or village. However,

by the 1870s, the railways had threaded their way across the country, and Bank Holidays and half-day Saturdays had been made obligatory by Act of Parliament. All of a sudden the ordinary working man and his family were able to enjoy days out and see a little more of the world.

With characteristic business acumen, Francis Frith foresaw that these new tourists would enjoy having souvenirs to commemorate their days out. In 1860 he married Mary Ann Rosling and set out with the intention of photographing every city, town and village in Britain. For the next thirty years he travelled the country by train and by pony and trap, producing fine photographs of seaside resorts and beauty spots that were keenly bought by millions of Victorians. These prints were painstakingly pasted into family albums and pored over during the dark nights of winter, rekindling precious memories of summer excursions.

The Rise of Frith & Co

Frith's studio was soon supplying retail shops all over the country. To meet the demand he gathered about him a small team of photographers, and published the work of independent artist-photographers of the calibre of Roger Fenton and Francis Bedford. In order to gain some understanding of the scale of Frith's business one only has to look at the catalogue issued by Frith & Co in 1886: it runs to some 670 pages, listing not only many thousands of views of the British Isles but also many photographs of most European countries, and China, Japan, the USA and Canada – note the sample page shown above from the hand-written *Frith & Co* ledgers detailing pictures taken. By 1890 Frith had created the greatest specialist photographic publishing company in the

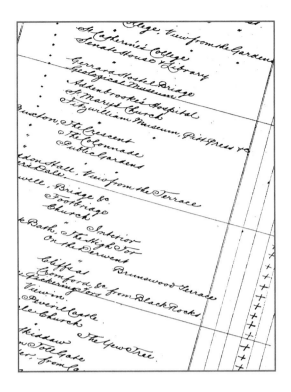

world, with over 2,000 outlets more than the combined number that Boots and W H Smith have today! The picture on the right shows the *Frith & Co* display board at Ingleton in the Yorkshire Dales. Beautifully constructed with mahogany frame and gilt inserts, it could display up to a dozen local scenes.

Postcard Bonanza

The ever-popular holiday postcard we know today took many years to develop. In 1870 the Post Office issued the first plain cards, with a pre-printed stamp on one face. In 1894 they allowed other publishers' cards to be sent through the mail with an attached adhesive halfpenny stamp. Demand grew rapidly, and in 1895 a new size of postcard was permitted called the court card, but there was little room for illustration. In 1899, a

year after Frith's death, a new card measuring 5.5 x 3.5 inches became the standard format, but it was not until 1902 that the divided back came into being, with address and message on one face and a full-size illustration on the other. *Frith & Co* were in the vanguard of postcard development, and Frith's sons Eustace and Cyril continued their father's monumental task, expanding the number of views offered to the public and recording more and more places in Britain, as the coasts and countryside were opened up to mass travel.

Francis Frith died in 1898 at his villa in Cannes, his great project still growing. The archive he created continued in business for another seventy years. By 1970 it contained over a third of a million pictures of 7,000 cities, towns and villages. The massive photographic record Frith has left to us stands as a living monument to a special and very remarkable man.

Frith's Archive: A Unique Legacy

FRANCIS FRITH'S legacy to us today is of immense significance and value, for the magnificent archive of evocative photographs he created provides a unique record of change in 7,000 cities, towns and villages throughout Britain over a century and more. Frith and his fellow studio photographers revisited locations many times down the years to update their views, compiling for us an enthralling and colourful pageant of British life and character.

We tend to think of Frith's sepia views of Britain as nostalgic, for most of us use them to conjure up memories of places in our own lives with which we have family associations. It often makes us forget that to Francis Frith they were records of daily life as it was actually being lived in the cities, towns and villages of his day. The Victorian age was one of great and often bewildering change for ordinary people, and though the pictures evoke an impression of slower times, life was as busy and hectic as it is today.

We are fortunate that Frith was a photographer of the people, dedicated to recording the minutiae of everyday life. For it is this sheer wealth of visual data, the painstaking chronicle of changes in dress, transport, street layouts, buildings, housing, engineering and landscape that captivates us so much today. His remarkable images offer us a powerful link with the past and with the lives of our ancestors.

Today's Technology

Computers have now made it possible for Frith's many thousands of images to be accessed almost instantly. In the Frith archive today, each photograph is carefully 'digitised' then stored on a CD Rom. Frith archivists can locate a single photograph amongst thousands within seconds. Views can be catalogued and sorted under a variety of categories of place and content to the immediate benefit of researchers.

Inexpensive reference prints can be created for them at the touch of a mouse button, and a wide range of books and other printed materials assembled and published for a wider, more general readership - in the next twelve months over a hundred Frith local history titles will be published! The day-to-day workings of the archive are very different from how they were in Francis Frith's time: imagine the herculean task of sorting through eleven tons of glass negatives as Frith had to do to locate a particular sequence of pictures!

See Frith at www.francisfrith.co.uk

Yet the archive still prides itself on maintaining the same high standards of excellence laid down by Francis Frith, including the painstaking cataloguing and indexing of every view.

It is curious to reflect on how the internet now allows researchers in America and elsewhere greater instant access to the archive than Frith himself ever enjoyed. Many thousands of individual views can be called up on screen within seconds on one of the Frith internet sites, enabling people living continents away to revisit the streets of their ancestral home town, or view places in Britain where they have enjoyed holidays. Many overseas researchers welcome the chance to view special theme selections, such as transport, sports, costume and ancient monuments.

We are certain that Francis Frith would have heartily approved of these modern developments in imaging techniques, for he himself was always working at the very limits of Victorian photographic technology.

The Value of the Archive Today

Because of the benefits brought by the computer, Frith's images are increasingly studied by social historians, by researchers into genealogy and ancestory, by architects, town planners, and by teachers and schoolchildren involved in local history projects.

In addition, the archive offers every one of us an opportunity to examine the places where we and our families have lived and worked down the years. Highly successful in Frith's own era, the archive is now, a century and more on, entering a new phase of popularity.

The Past in Tune with the Future

Historians consider the Francis Frith Collection to be of prime national importance. It is the only archive of its kind remaining in private ownership and has been valued at a million pounds. However, this figure is now rapidly increasing as digital technology enables more and more people around the world to enjoy its benefits.

Francis Frith's archive is now housed in an historic timber barn in the beautiful village of Teffont in Wiltshire. Its founder would not recognize the archive office as it is today. In place of the many thousands of dusty boxes containing glass plate negatives and an all-pervading odour of photographic chemicals, there are now ranks of computer screens. He would be amazed to watch his images travelling round the world at unimaginable speeds through network and internet lines.

The archive's future is both bright and exciting. Francis Frith, with his unshakeable belief in making photographs available to the greatest number of people, would undoubtedly approve of what is being done today with his lifetime's work. His photographs, depicting our shared past, are now bringing pleasure and enlightenment to millions around the world a century and more after his death.

Surrey - *An Introduction*

I MOVED TO CARSHALTON in 1959. At that time Carshalton was in Surrey, although the village was absorbed into Greater London in 1965 as part of the London Borough of Sutton. Accordingly I know the county well, and I cycled, walked and later rode my motorbike round its country lanes. I had friends as far afield as Dorking and relatives in Caterham, and then in Godstone and Reigate, and so I feel well qualified to write about the county in Francis Frith's 'Living Memories' series. In those days I was fascinated by the architecture of parish churches, and visited I think virtually all the interesting ones in the county, mostly by bike. Those I saw ranged from Chaldon, that splendid survival with its remarkable early 13th-century

Last Judgement wall paintings, standing high on Farthing Downs between Caterham in the east and Coulsdon/Hooley to the west, to Guildford Cathedral, which was still being built. This marvellously located building on a hill-top north-west of the town was designed in the 1930s, and its brickwork and its cool whitewashed interiors seemed to me at the time a creative development of the medieval Gothic styles. I remember my father, my brother and I watching six Spot Burnet moths fluttering amid the long grass near the chancel on a hot summer's day in about 1960, well before the surroundings were landscaped. My brother and I walked much of the North Downs. We used to go butterfly catching on Park Downs near

Chipstead, among whose village shops was a bakery where my father bought cream cakes as often as he dared.

So these are happy memories of my teens in Surrey. It is a county heavily influenced by London, and in reality the countryside we roamed in was preserved from further suburban sprawl only by the Metropolitan Green Belt, which was established just before World War II. This collection of views, exclusively from the 1950s and 1960s, shows the county before the redevelopment of town and village centres got under way, so in a sense the views are a record of a period dating from roughly the 1930s to the 1960s. After World War II there was a decade of relative inactivity. Indeed, that decade is remembered as one of universal drabness, as a bankrupted country struggled to regain prosperity and normality. Wartime rationing did not end until the mid 1950s on some products; I remember the extra rations we got for the Coronation in 1953, although I cannot recall what they were - I was only six at the time.

Surrey's modernisation, I suppose, came with Croydon (see my Francis Frith's 'Around Croydon: Living Memories') in the late 1950s, but in this book there is little sign of it elsewhere in the county; modernisation only got into full swing later in the 1960s. Addlestone received large civic offices and a 17-storey tower block of council flats in the early 1960s, and Guildford got the University of Surrey, built in modern style in 1968-9 and still continuing. After the early 1960s, Sutton and Kingston saw their biggest growth after their absorption into Greater London, so they fall outside the scope of this book. However, the influence of London shaped much of the county's expansion as commuter land. Woking, Camberley, Weybridge, Egham, Leatherhead, Epsom, Dorking, Redhill and Guildford owe much of their growth and prosperity to railway-borne commuters working in London and enjoying the countryside at weekends. I wish I could write that the new shopping centres and housing estates added to the architectural quality of the towns they descended upon, but it would be untrue. Desperate attempts to remedy the disasters by pedestrianising and traffic calming (Redhill is a good example of this) only serve to show up the poor quality of developer architecture.

By the 1980s standards were beginning to improve. More modern schemes have attempted to raise the quality and indeed to make best use of existing buildings, such as the Crown Court development in Godalming High Street or the Lion and Lamb Yard shopping centre in Farnham; but even recent supermarket buildings have shown the difficulty of integrating what are in effect vast sheds into historic towns, whatever the outer wall treatments. Some

towns, however, have avoided the worst excesses of the theory that rebuilding means survival and economic progress - and it has to be admitted that some towns had few good buildings to start with. For diplomatic reasons I will not name them.

In the 1950s Surrey still had villages with local workers, small post offices and pubs. The views in this book do show a lot of village post offices: this was always a popular theme with Frith's photographers, as postcards of local views were usually sold from the village post office. Nowadays village post offices are in rapid decline, but it is heartening that quite a few shown in this book still survive. Some of the High Streets must have disappointed Frith's roving photographers, for they are dull and architecturally poor, but others are excellent. One thing that has changed is the level of traffic in the county: being prosperous, Surrey has more two- and three-car families than any other English county, according to one local informant to whom I spoke. I can well believe it. Several villages and small towns in this book are now rendered less than pleasant, and crossing a road is a time-consuming operation for pedestrians. Prosperity has its downside.

My memories of leisure in early 1960s Surrey are also covered in this collection. They include the Wimpy Bar at Box Hill, a trendy arrival for young people then. It is still a beefburger chain with waitress (or waiter) service today, although the Box Hill branch has gone. Wimpy Bars were a trend dismissed by the older generation as creeping Americanisation on a par with the decadence of Elvis the Pelvis and rock and roll. More Spartan pleasures are represented by the view of Earlswood Lake with its seething mass of young swimmers, or of Frensham Little Pond with its boating and swimming. The 1950s and early 1960s were the last heyday of open-air swimming, whether in lakes or in rivers. We used to visit Guildford Lido with its large open-air pool and grassy surrounds for sun-bathing. The covered municipal swimming pool (such as the one at Walton-on-Thames of 1962-65) took over, although there had been covered ones before, such as Sutton's, which opened in 1903, or Malden Road Baths in North Cheam. From the 1970s these covered pools transmogrified into larger beasts - leisure centres were opened, such as the Arena in Camberley or the Cranleigh Leisure Centre.

The River Thames plays a significant role in the leisure of the north of the county, and there are a few views of it in this book. Other rivers and canals are significant, such as the now restored Basingstoke Canal or the Wey Navigation, and the rivers Wey and Mole and their tributaries. The view of Tilford at the end of Chapter 4 shows the River Wey as a summer leisure facility (to use modern jargon), while in

Chapter 1 there are views with boating as the leisure theme. Today, Surrey in effect provides homes for commuters, both to London and to the larger commercial centres within the county such as Guildford or Woking, while its countryside and water provides leisure for this population. There is a sense of this already in several of the views in the book, but the use of the countryside for leisure is much more marked now. Long-distance waymarked footpaths pass through Surrey, such as the North Downs Way, the Thames Path, the London Countryway and the Greensand Way. Box Hill has been a noted beauty spot for many years, and so has Leith Hill; their popularity shows no sign of diminishing.

I do not wish to give the impression that all change was for the worse, or that Surrey vanished from view. This book includes many views of a Surrey that has physically changed little since the 1960s (or indeed much since the 19th century). The book also has several of the county's deservedly popular show-pieces, such as Chiddingfold with its splendid green surrounded by exceptionally good historic houses and cottages, Bletchingley with its fine church and wide former market place, Ockley along the old Roman road of Stane Street, Coldharbour nestling at the foot of Leith Hill, Brockham with its village green, East Clandon with its numerous timber-framed cottages, and

the popular villages of Shere, Puttenham, Chobham and others. Surrey also boasts some fine towns, whose character survives well in some cases - and patchily in others, unfortunately. This selection includes Reigate, Dorking, Godalming, Haslemere, Farnham and Guildford. Again, traffic is a problem, particularly in Reigate and Farnham, and gets in the way of full enjoyment of the townscape.

Thus we have two Surreys: the suburban fringe to London, where change has been most intense, and then the barrier of the chalk North Downs with their steep southern escarpment. Towns and villages occupy many of the dry valleys or the river valleys that cut through the chalk, and immediately south of the escarpment is a string of villages and towns that includes Dorking, Godstone, Reigate and Haslemere. Guildford makes spectacular use of the chalk ridge where the Wey cuts through it, but the Downs and the Hog's Back do form a barrier; the best villages and hamlets are south of it in the greensand hills and on the edge of the Weald. To the south-west, around Friday Street and Holmbury St Mary, the greensand scenery is heavily wooded; the county (and south-east England) reaches its highest point above sea level at Leith Hill. This is rolling countryside with deep-cut valleys. The north-west of the county has a character of its own, with thousands of acres of heathland, pine woods and lakes and

ponds on the Bagshot sands - examples are Frensham Great and Little Pond and the pine heaths thereabouts. Other areas, oddly enough, are preserved by being used as army firing ranges, like Pirbright Common or Westend Common.

I hope this selection captures the character of the Surrey I remember from the late 1950s to the mid 1960s with all its suburban and rural contrasts, from suburban shopping parades to village post offices, from historic town centres to 20th century developments, from canals to river banks, and from leafy greensand hills to leafy suburbia: it is a county of remarkable differences in such a small compass. Within its boundaries, roughly 40 miles by 30 deep at the west and tapering to 15 miles in the east, over a million people live: it is no wonder that its 420,000 acres generate huge amounts of traffic. While researching this book, I think I met most of Surrey's population in their cars; but it is still possible to find peace and quiet here. I have great affection for Surrey, and I hope this collection of Frith views shows why.

The London and Suburban Influences

Egham
The King's Head c1950 E27011

This first chapter is a tour from west to east in the parts of
Surrey most affected by London. We start in Egham, a town on
higher ground south of the River Thames. Unlike Staines on the
north bank, the river plays no part in Egham's townscape. This
view looks east along the High Street. The King's Head has
gone for a 1960s parade of shops with flats over, Arndale
House, while much on the left has also been rebuilt. The bus
stop site is now the start of the sweeping Church Way inner
relief road running behind the Arndale development.

Egham
The Roundway c1950 E27002

Egham is not the most inspiring of Surrey towns. This view is at the east end of the High Street at the roundabout where it joins the A30, in effect the northern by-pass. The buildings on the left survive, as does the church, although now converted to flats as Winslade House. The Eclipse pub on the right, built in typical Surrey 1930s road-house vernacular, is now a Caffe Uno. The site of the Hoover repairers with the petrol pumps visible beyond has been replaced by a large BP garage.

Stanwell, The Rising Sun c1965 S588009

In 1965, when Greater London was created, Surrey crossed the River Thames and gained a segment of the former county of Middlesex. This segment included Stanwell, whose village centre has quite a few good buildings and a church with a strikingly good tower. This view is north of the village, looking south across the 16th-century Duke of Northumberland's River with the southern perimeter road to Heathrow Airport immediately behind the photographer. The other bridge crosses Longford River, and beyond is the Rising Sun pub.

Sunbury, Thames Street c1955 S248027

Sunbury was also in Middlesex until 1965. Here Frith's photographer looks east along Thames Street in Lower Sunbury. The houses on the right, including The Little House facing the camera (and now painted a bright pink), have the River Thames as their south boundary. The road runs alongside the river, and an ait, or island, lies beside the trees in the distance. The mansard-roofed building on the left is now a Café Rouge, and the shops are now houses.

Laleham, Chertsey Lock c1960 L5058
West of Sunbury and on the former Middlesex bank of the Thames is Chertsey Lock, near Chertsey Bridge, an austere seven-arch stone bridge of the 1780s by James Paine. Thames Side Road is on the right with a mobile home park beyond, while on the left in the distance is now the blue steel bridge that carries the M3 over the river.

Chertsey, London Street c1955 C80027
Chertsey was once the town at the gates of one of the most powerful abbeys in England. Chertsey Abbey was founded in 666 AD and has now almost completely vanished; much of its stonework was used at Henry VIII's Hampton Court after the Dissolution of the Monasteries. The main east-west street of the town - Windsor Street this side of the Town Hall and London Street beyond - is indeed dominated by the 1851 Town Hall, which projects over the pavement; it is now a restaurant called Bar 163.

Chertsey
Guildford Street c1955 C80026
At right angles to Windsor Street, Guildford Street has seen many changes since the 1950s. In the distance in this view looking north are the trees of St Peter's parish churchyard. The 18th-century King's Head Hotel survives, and so do the shops to the right, a 1930s parade, and a few shops beyond the hotel, but there has been much injudicious rebuilding from the 1960s onwards. To the left, out of shot, is the Sainsbury Centre, a shopping mall with the eponymous supermarket at the end.

Virginia Water
The Waterfall c1960 V4006

This evocative photograph is taken west of Chertsey on the A30 London Road at its junction with Christchurch Road, the B389, which lies beyond the policeman on points duty and to the left of the white-painted building. This was built in the 1930s under the influence of the Modern Movement, and it is a building of surpassing ugliness; it has a café with a terrace, the Waterfall, and below a Rover and Jaguar car dealer, Gavin Fairfax. It survives as a Chiquito's Restaurant. Its style owes something to the Wentworth Estate to the south-west, where there are many houses in a similar style, but mostly better than this.

Addlestone, Station Road c1955 A23003

Addlestone grew up in the mid 19th century with the arrival of the railway, when a few villas and many more terraces and pairs of artisan houses were built. The town was greatly augmented by 20th-century suburban housing, but architecturally it is the poor relation of Weybridge and Chertsey. Station Road, behind the photographer, is the main shopping street, and now has two major supermarkets. The station is to the left of the footbridge, which remains today; but the level crossing gates have been replaced by automatic barriers, and the villa went for blocks of flats.

Addlestone, High Street c1955 A23027

The High Street is distinctly low-key: the terraces of late Victorian shops are augmented by 1930s buildings, as we see on the left, and now several have been converted to take-aways. At the crossroads the High Street meets Station Road, while just to the left of the view are some neo-Georgian flats of the 1970s. Just left of the crossroads, in Station Road, are Runnymede Civic Offices. Beyond is a 17-storey 1960s tower block of council flats, an incongruous intrusion into low-rise Addlestone.

Ottershaw, The Otter Corner c1955 O26013
We are west of Addlestone. Here the A320 Guildford Road meets the A319 Chobham Road and the B3121, Murray Road, from Addlestone at what is now a large roundabout. The Otter pub, a 1930s Surrey vernacular-style road-house, has now been transformed into a farmyard complex: the upper floor of the main block has been white clap-boarded and given a tiled lean-to veranda, while extensions to the left read like farm buildings and culminate in a fake oast house - picturesque and fun.

New Haw, Woodham Lane c1965 N183016
This is Surrey suburbia par excellence. Woodham Lane, between New Haw and Woodham, is semi-detached country served by two railway stations: Byfleet and New Haw, and West Byfleet. On the right is Grange Parade; the right block was built in 1934, the left in 1935. Beyond is the Black Prince pub and then a garage, as usual built in a non-Tudor style with white render and flat roofs, influenced by the Modern Movement, to reflect the motor car's different image.

West Byfleet
Rosemount Parade c1960 W456007
West Byfleet is more stylish with its architecturally-considered parade of shops and flats: this is quite a successful composition, with occasional timber-framed accents. At the far end a bank in Wren/Queen Anne style completes the row. Across the road beyond is a good Art Nouveau/Gothic church of 1912. Thus West Byfleet at least tried to create a Garden Suburb feel, but later development and redevelopment let things go rather.

Byfleet
High Road 1951 B265025

East of the M25 and the older River Wey Navigation, Byfleet is a suburban village; although it is built along winding lanes, it is architecturally disappointing. At its east end, down by the River Wey, is a superb brick manor house of the 1680s, which has been much altered subsequently and is now divided into apartments. Back in the village centre, things are less coherent. The Lloyds TSB bank (right) in Bedford Park style of 1879 promised greater things than its dismal surroundings in the High Road.

Byfleet, Chertsey Road c1965 B265046
Further north, at the A245 Parvis Road junction, the photographer looks back down High Road with Lloyds TSB on the left and the Dutch-gabled fire station of 1885 on the right, complete with its siren tower (now gone). Candy Corner gave way to an office block in the 1980s. In the distance is Amptwade House of 1905 with mock timber gables, now Boutell and Son, funeral directors. To the left is the old Civic Restaurant, which we will see in view B265022.

Byfleet, The Civic Restaurant c1955 B265022
The Civic Restaurant was also the village hall. It was built in 1898 to commemorate Queen Victoria's Diamond Jubilee in a typical domestic Tudor revival style with a timber-framed upper floor, a cupola and battlemented stair turrets - an attractive composition. Byfleet Village Hall also now houses Byfleet Parish Council offices, and is currently under repair (October 2001).

**Weybridge
Queens Road c1955**
W74025
Weybridge is famous for its suburb for the very rich, St George's Hill. There is more to Weybridge, but it is somewhat disappointing: occasional islands of quality amid suburbia from all periods from the mid 19th century. Monument Green is perhaps the best bit, along with the road down to the river from the town centre; the monument dates from 1694, and was relocated from Seven Dials by Convent Garden. This view shows the shopping parades on Queens Road, mostly later 19th century with rather better 1930s additions to the left.

Walton-on-Thames High Street c1955

W19016

Walton-on-Thames is another suburbanised town south-west of London along the River Thames. Built on slightly higher land away from the river, it turns its back on it, and this view looks north-west along the High Street to the Church Street crossroads. There is the usual suburban shopping street mix of timber-framed mock Tudor, neo-Georgian and Victorian architecture. The tall building centre left is the Art Deco-ish Burton's - its foundation stones were laid by members of the family in 1938 - and on the right is W H Smith in a heavily-corniced neo-Georgian style.

Walton on Thames
The Riverside c1955 W19002
By the river, a road leads off Walton Lane under the bridge
towards Walton Marina. At weekends the banks are lively with
visitors, strollers and walkers, rowing club members, and people
visiting the café. The warehouses beyond the bridge have gone, to
be replaced by blocks of flats in Swan Walk and Riverside which
take advantage of the river views. However, their view is marred
at present (October 2001) by what I hope is a temporary road
bridge - the 1860s one in this view has been demolished.

Molesey Lock, The Lock c1955 M88001
Further downstream and opposite Hampton Court, Molesey Lock is photographed from Riverbank, the busy A3050 along the Surrey bank of the River Thames. The lock, built in 1814, was rebuilt in 1906 specifically to accommodate naval vessels up to 200 feet long built on Platt's Eyot further upstream. However, from the 1880s its most frequent use was for pleasure craft, as we see here. By the road is a rather good war memorial, while to the east there are views of Hampton Court Palace and the 1930s river bridge, designed partly by Lutyens.

Thames Ditton, High Street c1955 T103011
The best part of Thames Ditton architecturally is north and west of this viewpoint, which shows the post office at the High Street's junction with Ashley Road. The lime tree on the right has been replaced by another, and the post office is still here, its roughcast now painted white. Leonard North's garage has gone, to be replaced by a pair of Surrey vernacular-style cottages. The parade to the left survives. Beyond are two of the big houses that line the north end of the High Street, mostly late Georgian and earlier 19th-century.

▼ **Long Ditton, Portsmouth Road c1955** L457004

This view, along the Portsmouth Road, formerly the A3, shows the late Victorian expansion of Kingston past Surbiton. The shopping parade is in Dutch revival style, built before Surrey discovered the mock timber-frame leitmotif for its shopping parades - it dates from around 1900. Past the junction with St Leonards Road is a block of 1930s flats, St Leonards Court, and beyond that pairs of 1930s semis. Opposite, out of view to the left, are earlier Victorian and Edwardian semis.

▼ **Claygate, The Parade 1952** C519018

Claygate lies southwards beyond the A3 Kingston and Esher by-pass, and into the preserved countryside of the Green Belt. The village grew up firstly when Thames Ditton's commons were enclosed in 1838, and then when the railway arrived in 1885. Frith's photographer looks from the railway station along The Parade, which was started soon after the railway arrived. Station Buildings on the left chose the gabled style, and are earlier than the more architecturally developed styles opposite. At the end the vista across Hare Lane is closed by the 1930s Westminster Bank, now a travel agency, and trees.

▲ **Cobham, High Street c1955** C131012

Cobham is architecturally not the equal of the similarly named Chobham. This view captures well the disparate suburban nature of Cobham's High Street before we reach the most attractive River Hill and Mill Road, which stretch along the banks of the River Mole. There has been much rebuilding of this part of the High Street, none of it for the better, since the 1950s; continuity has been achieved only by the building at the far left, which is still an estate agency.

◀ **Ewell, High Street c1955**
E45048
East from Claygate and across the Hogsmill river valley, the route reaches Ewell, now by-passed by the A24 London to Worthing road. The town preserves its High Street well at the north end and along Church Street, a turning off it; both streets contain timber-framed and later Georgian houses of quality. This view, though, is of the south end, which has fared less well: typical suburban mock-Tudor shopping parades proliferate both on the left and out of view to the right and behind the camera.

Epsom
High Street c1955
E37047
Epsom is another Surrey town that has suffered from over-enthusiastic redevelopment in the 1960s. This view looks west from an upper window of the Spread Eagle at the Ashley Road crossroads along the High Street towards the clock tower, built in 1847 and no architectural masterpiece. Most of the buildings in the middle distance have now been replaced, but the ones nearer the camera survive, including the tall 1897 Post Office.

◄ **Ashtead**
The Street c1955 A72017
The medieval parish church, Ashtead Park house and its landscaped park, now part of the City of London Freemen's School, are south of this main through road, the A24 London to Worthing road. The high street, known as The Street, was mostly Victorian in character, but has been rebuilt; some houses on the left beyond the single-storey shops went up in the 1960s. Barclays Bank is now a restaurant and take-away, while Westminster Bank on the right is offices. The chemist next to it remains a chemist, Lloyds Pharmacy.

◄ Epsom
Derby Day c1955 E37012

Epsom is famous for two things: Epsom Salts, and the two great classic flat races run on the Downs south of the town, the Derby and the Oaks, both inaugurated in the late 18th century. The salts gave the town its first fame in the 17th century as a noted spa town, but the May race meeting still remains immensely popular and draws huge crowds. This view shows the bookies doing a roaring trade. Note the William Hill hoarding: this is still a major firm of turf accountants today.

▼ Ashtead
The Fish Pond c1955 A72011

In the 1920s and 1930s, Ashtead expanded northwards towards Ashtead Common. This view was taken at the crossroads of Woodfield Road, Barnett Wood Lane and Craddocks Parade, the 1930s three-storey flats over shops. In the foreground is the ancient pond, once known as Oxmoor Pond, which lies in a stretch of green that is the southernmost outpost of Ashtead Common. The trees and park on the left across the road are the salient from the common into the suburbia of Lower Ashtead.

◄ Tadworth
Cross Road c1955 T1004

Back past Epsom Downs, the route reaches Tadworth, a station on the Tattenham Corner branch line from Purley; it is part of the suburban development that spreads from Tadworth north-east through Burgh Heath and Nork to Banstead. The station, which opened in 1900, is to the left of the photographer, who is focusing on the 1930s mock-Tudor shopping parade with its striking row of gables. The heavily-pruned limes have now gone, but the two pine trees on the left survive.

Drift Bridge
The Cross Roads c1955 D221001
Back past Tattenham Corner station, the route descends to Drift
Bridge, the name deriving from the sheep-droving past of this now
suburban area. Nowadays much 'improved', this 1950s view looks
across from Fir Tree Road, now the A2022 to Banstead, to the
1930s mock-Tudor shopping parade on the road that climbs up to
Epsom Downs and the race course. The big trees have now gone,
and so has the pedimented petrol station, to be replaced by a late
1990s Volkswagen dealership.

Drift Bridge, The Parade c1955 D221022
The photographer has gone uphill to look past the shopping parade in all its mock-Tudor timber-framed glory to the crossroads with Reigate Road and Fir Tree Road opposite. Note the old police telephone box by the junction.

Nork, The Parade c1955 N184008
Nork is a suburb that merges south into Burgh Heath in the large triangle between Reigate Road, Brighton Road and Fir Tree Road, the north boundary of Nork. The Parade is Nork's local shopping centre, a left turn off Fir Tree Road; Eastgate on the left, out of camera shot, has large three-storey blocks of 1930s flats. Again there is continuity: the right-hand shop is still an estate agency, and the newsagents in the distance still sells newspapers.

▼ Nork, The Golf Club c1955 N184023

North of Fir Tree Road and just beyond Banstead railway station is Cuddington Park Golf Course; the name is a reminder of the parish and village of Cuddington, which was cleared for Henry VIII's Nonsuch Palace. East of this golf course is the Banstead Downs Golf Course, and then east of the railway lies the rest of Banstead Downs, which are undeveloped heath and woodland. The golf club house, a rather distinguished Lutyens-esque Surrey vernacular revival building, has expanses of tiled roofs and a rather grand entrance bay with golden sandstone dressings. It opened on 1 January 1929.

▼ Banstead, The Station c1965 B391114

Banstead station, on the branch line from Sutton to Epsom Downs station, opened in 1865. The stucco house on the left, most recently Banstead Builders Merchants, dates from around that time, while the station building retains some of the 1865 work. The kiosk is now a builder's office, and the station building is let as offices. Chimneyless now, the roof is no longer painted with giant letters. The station is nearly a mile from the town centre of Banstead.

▲ Burgh Heath Brighton Road c1955

B723005

Burgh Heath is very suburban, and its east side is blighted by the roaring traffic of the dual carriageway A217 Reigate road, which merges with the A23 Brighton road at Horley, south of Redhill. This view is taken from south of the Reigate Road and Brighton Road junction, with Brighton Road running uphill in the centre of the view. The shopping parade with flats over is unchanged, but the fir tree and the walls to the left have gone for road improvements. There is now a large Shell garage just out of picture to the left.

◀ **Burgh Heath**
The Sugar Bowl c1955
B723020
The Sugar Bowl stands south of the junction with Reigate Road, on the east side of the road. In the 1950s it was a restaurant offering morning coffee, luncheons, teas and dinners, and architecturally no great shakes; it has since been heavily modernised, and is now Heathside, a family restaurant, with a large block behind, a Premier Lodge hotel. The upper storey is now tile-hung and shorn of its oriel windows, half-timbered dormers and chimneys.

**Banstead
High Street c1955**
B391013
Banstead's High Street
was mostly rebuilt from
the 1920s on with
shopping parades; it
has a completely
suburban character,
except for the parish
churchyard of All Saints
on the right of this view
amid the trees. The
bare looking lime tree
in the middle distance
on the left is beside
where the village pond
once was, while the
buildings beyond have
since been replaced.

Woodmansterne
The Village c1955 W507011

From Banstead the route heads east to Woodmansterne. Here we are not looking at the hamlet along Woodmansterne Street, but at the junction of Rectory Lane and Chipstead Valley Road that winds along the valley floor from suburban Purley to the village of Tadworth. Yet another 1930s mock-Tudor shopping parade leads downhill to Chipstead Valley Road. Here stand the buildings of the Woodmansterne Treatment Works, a fine complex of Queen Anne-style pedimented buildings of 1907, now belonging to the Sutton and East Surrey Water company.

Chipstead, High Road c1965 C484045
The older parts of Chipstead village are on the chalk ridge above the dry valley some 150 feet below, along which Chipstead Valley Road runs. This view on High Road looks south past the Starrock Lane turning towards the Hazelwood Lane turning to the right. The shop has gone, to be replaced by a pair of semis, while the shop on the far right, dated 1885, is now the premises of a cabinet maker and furniture restorer.

Hooley, The Shopping Centre c1965 H438301
Descending from Chipstead into the next valley east brings us to Hooley. It was long known to motorists on the A23 London to Brighton road for the major hold-ups at its traffic light junction with Star Lane, just out of view to the left. This photograph looks north past the garage, now rebuilt as a BP petrol station. Beyond is the almost inevitable Surrey mock-Tudor half-timbered shopping parade. Fords, the newsagent and tobacconists, is now Hooley Newsagents and Post Office, and the café has migrated to the end building.

Chaldon, St Lawrence's Hospital c1965 C482003
This stretch of country used to have three major hospitals, the most famous of which was Cane Hill, built as a lunatic asylum in 1882. St Lawrence's Hospital, to the west of Caterham and east of the tiny hill hamlet of Chaldon, was built in 1869 as the Metropolitan Asylum for London's insane; it accommodated 1,000 men and 1,200 women in its vast ranges of buildings, seen on the left in this view. The early 1960s buildings in the foreground were added for a school for children with learning difficulties. All has been swept away since, to be replaced by housing estates. The hospital's name is preserved in a road name: St Lawrence Way.

Warlingham, The Village c1955 W27027
This chapter finishes across the next valley and up on the chalk ridge at Warlingham, 600 feet above sea level. At the centre of this village, which is attached by suburbia to Purley and Croydon, is a triangular green with a war memorial. The Green is out of view to the right; the buildings we see here are on its north side - the houses are dated 1898. Beyond the contemporary Warlingham Church Hall are 1920s shops and a bank, which is dated 1927.

A Tour of South-East Surrey

Oxted
The Hoskins Arms Hotel c1955 O35008

The second tour starts in Oxted, where all is not as it seems. The original village, cut off by the by-pass, is to the west; while this photograph, taken from the junction with Easthill Road, shows the corner of Station Road West. In the 1920s the lord of the manor, Charles Hoskins Master, laid out the road to the railway station and built spectacularly convincing timber-framed shops with flats over. Caxton House on the right, now the Stamp Shop, is an example. Opposite is the 1890s hotel, replaced in the 1990s by blocks of flats, The Hoskins. Out of view to the left is Master Park, a public park established by Charles Master in 1923.

▼ Blindley Heath, The Main Road c1955 B123004

South-west of Oxted, and on the course of a Roman Road across the Weald, the route turns left at Blindley Heath, a hamlet on former heathland in the south of Godstone parish. Most of the houses are 19th-century, including the shop (dated 1881) on the corner of Ray Lane beyond the now relocated war memorial cross. It is now a private house called The Old Post Office. The building behind the Ediswan Lamps sign has gone - a Texaco garage now stands on the site.

▼ Blindley Heath, The Red Barn c1955 B123001

On Ray Lane, the road to Lingfield, at its junction with Tandridge Lane, stands The Red Barn; in the 1950s it offered luncheon, teas and dinners to travellers. It makes a picturesque composition behind its pond. The barn itself is no longer agricultural, and has been added to the restaurant: nowadays it offers 'The Family Welcome', and there is a huge car park to the right of this view. The house was built as a 15th-century open hall house, but it was altered in the 17th century.

▲ Lingfield
The Old Prison and the Pond c1955 L50009

This village is a disappointment: its good bits are separated by development that started when the railway arrived in the 1880s. This view shows one of the most picturesque areas apart from the church. Admittedly, the Old Cage, the village lock-up or prison, looks like a miniature church. Its date is disputed - some consider it an 18th-century confection made from older stone. The village pond, the prison, the ancient hollow oak and the cottages nearby all remain today.

◄ **Lingfield
Godstone Road c1955**
L50038
This view looks from Godstone Road to the Plaistow Street-Newchapel Road junction. The Esso petrol pumps have gone, and the huts and the cottage on the right have now been replaced by a Total garage (the chimneys beyond belong to Ormuz Cottages, dated 1894). The mock-Tudor shopping parade is of about 1900, and The Mart, the third shop from the left, is still The Mart, a newsagent, tobacconist and confectioner. This view shows rather well the somewhat disjointed architecture of the village.

Dormansland, The Post Office c1965 D46017
Immediately south-east of Lingfield lies the race course, founded in 1890, and beyond that is the next station on the railway line, Dormans. It opened in 1884, and Dormans Park was laid out with houses in treed plots - the roads are still gravelled. The village itself expanded too, but here there were older buildings, such as the Post Office, seen here amid an irregular terrace of brick and tile-hanging. Down the road is the Sussex border and East Grinstead.

Outwood, The Post Office c1965 O29016
Back to the west of Blindley Heath the route reaches Outwood, a hamlet on the edge of heath and woodland, some of it owned by the National Trust. The major landmark is the windmill, a post mill dated 1665. The old post office looked across the green towards it - indeed, the cottage next to the shop is called Windmill Cottage (the right-hand half is Forge Cottage). The post office is now a house, The Gallery.

Bletchingley
The Morning of the Hunt c1945 B122029

Going north to the Godstone to Reigate road, that part of the A25
that runs along the greensand ridge south of the North Downs, we
reach the village of Bletchingley. Here the photographer looks
west along the High Street from the junction with Outwood Lane
on the morning of a fox hunt - this type of scene was much
favoured for Frith postcards. It is a fine High Street architecturally,
and is given all the more impact by its climbing and curving.

▼ **Bletchingley, The Church c1955** B122030

Off the north side of the High Street, the buildings are encroachments on the market place; Bletchingley had been a borough by the 13th century. The back lane alongside the church follows the original north edge of the market place. Bletchingley also had a castle, which was destroyed in 1264, and from 1285 to 1832 it had MPs. The church is a good one - the tower is basically Norman. The shop on the left is now an antique lighting shop, while the garage has gone, to be replaced by a clothes shop.

▼ **Bletchingley, The Hunt at Ye Olde Whyte Hart Hotel c1965** B122083

The 1890s terrace with its four gabled full-height bay windows steps down the hill; the left-hand one on the corner of Outwood Lane is now no longer a Barclays Bank, but the offices of financial consultants. The Whyte Harte has a rendered and colourwashed front over a Tudor timber-frame (it may be earlier: there is a date, 1388, on the building), and it is obviously the supplier of stirrup cups to the hunt before it moves off.

▲ **Godstone
The Village Green
c1955** G27030

Until the M25 and M23 by-passed Godstone, it had become seriously blighted by traffic on the Eastbourne road, the A22 and east-west traffic on the A25, which peaked in the 1960s and 1970s. It is still busy, of course, but much more endurable, and the village has regained much of its quality of life. This tranquil scene, with a cricket match in full swing on the village green, looks towards the south side of the green; the A22 is on the far left beyond the trees.

◄ **Caterham**
Godstone Road c1955
C49009
Caterham is in two parts, up the hill where the medieval church is, and Caterham Valley to the east on the valley floor, which grew up when the railway arrived in 1856 - it was in fact a terminus station. Thus the lower town is Victorian in character, with later suburbs, and its church, St John's, dates from the 1880s. Until the eastern by-pass was built the main A22 poured through the centre, and this roundabout was extremely busy. Here we look south along Godstone Road, with the church tower on the right.

**Caterham
Godstone Road c1955**
C49057
This view looks back towards the roundabout, with Croydon Road beyond. The double-gabled building on the right dates from 1888, and the railings and tree on the left belong to a small green alongside the road leading to the church. The buildings in the far distance have been replaced by Quadrant House, a long three-storey white-painted flat-roofed range of shops and flats built in 1966.

◀ **Redhill**
High Street c1955 R17007
Redhill grew from nothing after the
building of the London to Brighton
road in 1807 and the railway in 1841.
Thus in the 1950s the town has a
mainly Victorian character, although
not a very distinguished one. This view
of the High Street, looking south from
the Station Road crossroads, changed
dramatically when the M23 and M25
by-passed the town; much has been
pedestrianised and demolished.
Fortunately the Wheatsheaf of 1900
on the right survives as an O'Neills
pub, and so does the former Burton's
on the opposite corner, but most of
the right-hand buildings have gone for
the Belfry Shopping Centre.

◄ Merstham
High Street c1955 M67017

Moving west, the route passes through Merstham, a village of two parts: the older part lies west of the railway, and to its east is a large former London County Council housing estate of the 1950s, now with the vast M25/M23 junction nearby. Frith's photographer has wisely turned his camera on the old village. This view looks north along the High Street, which curves to the right; the cottages beyond Merstham Garage are in Quality Street. The main loss in this view is the gabled stone hall on the right, while the garage has been rebuilt, still retaining the 1796 cottage.

▼ Redhill
The Earlswood Lakes c1955
R17303

South of the Redhill/Reigate built-up areas are the Earlswood Lakes, which lie in the midst of the grassy heathland of Earlswood Common. I remember swimming there in the 1950s, and learning to ride motor-cycles with the ACU in the early 1960s on the roads of the Earlswood sewage farm to the south of the lakes. Nowadays the diving tower has gone, fishermen line the banks, and there are notices along the edge of the lake warning of the dangers of deep water!

◄ Earlswood
Horley Road c1955 E1029

This uninspiring view looks south along the A23 London to Brighton road, which was completed in 1807; it is now lined by late Victorian and Edwardian semis on the right with 1920s housing on the left. The oddly inappropriately-named Clearview Filling Station has been replaced by a modern Shell garage. Mollie's Transport Café has gone, to be replaced by modern flats, Mayfield Court, and the road is now a dual carriageway.

▼ Salfords, The Prince Albert c1965 S45009

The Prince Albert stands further south on Horley Road, actually in South Earlsfield rather than Salfords, and north of the junction of Horley Road with Woodhatch Road. It dates from about 1850, when Prince Albert was at the height of his popularity. Built in coursed chalk with brick dressings, its bow windows were added in the 1950s. Recently the upper floor has been clad in shiplap boarding. At present (October 2001) the Prince Albert is closed and undergoing refurbishment.

▼ Nutfield, The Post Office and the Street c1955 N53003

East of Redhill, on the A25, Nutfield is still heavy with traffic, despite the M25 by-passing it to the north. Like Bletchingley, the village is on the greensand ridge which the A25 follows for much of its length. As with many other villages in Surrey, the shops have either become houses (the one on the left with the blinds is now The Old Bakery), or secondary commercial premises - the post office on the right is now the Grace Barnard Design Centre.

▲ South Nutfield The Village c1955

S666001

A mile south of Nutfield, a new village grew up around the railway station on the Tonbridge line named South Nutfield. This view is taken looking along Station Approach north from beside the station; at this date, the shops and houses are almost unchanged since they were built in the 1890s. Now the pace of change has accelerated: the shopfronts in Station Parade have been renewed, and Southgate's is now Parade Stores and Post Office.

◄ **Reigate**
High Street c1955 R20067
Reigate town is considerably more attractive than Redhill, with which it is now merged by development. It contains some good townscape, but it is somewhat traffic-blighted, more so now than in this 1950s view, which looks east along the High Street towards Market Square. The building with the clock turret and cupola is the old Town Hall of 1728. The town was of some significance in the Middle Ages with a castle, a borough charter, a fine parish church and an Augustinian priory.

Reigate
Church Street c1955 R20007
This view looks east from the upper windows of the old Town Hall
along Church Street. This street is of lesser architectural quality
than the High Street, with much neo-Georgian rebuilding on the
right, including Barclays Bank. There are shopping parades of the
neo-Georgian two storeys of flat-over-shops types built later in the
1950s beyond (a building site in this view). On the left the Market
Hotel survives, and so does the building beyond, which is now a
Café Rouge. This chapter's tour concludes here.

Central Surrey South and East of Guildford

Shalford
The Village c1955 S101010

Our third tour starts in Shalford, in effect a suburb of Guildford on the east side of the River Wey where the Tillingbourne meets it. The church and the old core of the village are further north, but this view is along King's Road with the common to the right of the rider. The post office survives here, with the garage converted to be part of it, while the rather fine late Victorian butcher's shopfront to the right has now been rebuilt as Wing Hung Chinese restaurant.

▼ Wonersh, The Village c1955 W127002

South-east of Shalford, Wonersh has an old core with some fine timber-framed houses, including the 16th-century Grantley Arms pub; there are more old houses along the winding The Street, which starts to the right of this view. This quaint combined signpost and sheltered seat stands at the junction with The Street, Kings Road and Cranleigh Road. It is a 1920s delight, and reminiscent of a market cross in miniature.

▼ Shamley Green, The Village and the Post Office c1965 S103058

Moving south-east and still within Wonersh parish, we reach Shamley Green, in 1965 still a remote Surrey hamlet loosely built around its triangular green. Nowadays it is much smarter and more prosperous. L T Gamblin's village smithy with the cycles leaning against it has gone the way of most forges and is now a shop, Poppy's Delicatessen, while the post office is now the Beauty Gallery and has lost its telephone kiosk. Note the bubble car - a real period piece.

▲ Cranleigh High Street c1955

C180008

It is difficult to connect the town of Cranleigh with its name, which means 'clearing of the herons, or cranes'. Although it retains some villagey characteristics, and was once important in the Wealden iron industry, it is very much nowadays a small town. The foreground in this view is now occupied by a roundabout and Village Way, which leads off to the right and the Cranleigh Leisure Centre.

◀ **Cranleigh**
The Village Hall c1955
C180030
View C180008 was taken in front of the village hall. It is dated 1935, and is a large timber-framed building of some quality, convincingly done. Village Way now passes to its left to the Leisure Centre and its car parks. The buildings to the right have been demolished, and are replaced by a modern shopping centre with the upper floor tile-hung in Surrey vernacular style.

◀ **Forest Green
The Common c1955** F39012
Moving east towards Leith
Hill, but still south of the
woodland that covers the
greensand hills, the tour
reaches Forest Green, a
hamlet scattered around an
extensive green. This view east
of the 1897 church shows the
cottages and the post office,
now closed; the telephone
box has been removed and
the post office converted to a
house, called unsurprisingly
The Old Post House East. The
cricket pitch beyond the last
house was laid out in the
1920s on part of the common.

◄ **Ewhurst**
Deblins Green c1965 E47090
This small green is at the north end of the village - the Bull's Head pub stands on the left out of the picture. This view looks to the west side of the square green, with the bellcote of the Evangelical Church in the distance. To the right, the tile-hung Deblins Green with its hipped tiled roof and tile-hung upper floor dates from about 1700. To the right, Jack Bennett's Esso garage (later renamed Pitt's Garage) recently closed, and the tiled pump canopy and the pumps were removed. Its good timber-framed house behind remains; it is currently awaiting repair (October 2001).

▼ **Ockley**
Stane Street c1955 O7015
Ockley is a very fine village along the course of the Roman road from London to Chichester, which has been known from Anglo-Saxon times as Stane Street. The village is in places built hard up to the road (now the A29) as in this view, or along the edge of long greens, while the parish church is half a mile east of the village. The Old Hatch, the cross-winged house on the left, has heavy Horsham sandstone roof slates. The petrol station on the right has been replaced by a 1970s pair of houses.

◄ **Capel**
The King's Head c1955
C20024
This is yet another building that has changed since the 1960s. The King's Head in The Street in Capel, a village now by-passed by the A24 London to Worthing road, is now a private house, and its once sterile car park is now an attractive front garden. Presumably, the by-pass killed the pub's trade. The tile-hung left part is 16th-century, and the then smart right-hand block is early 19th-century.

◄ **Coldharbour Main Street c1955**

C137031

A little further on is the Plough, which we can see on the right behind the telephone kiosk (which is still there). The lane behind Frith's photographer becomes the track up to Leith Hill. Behind the pub and the house rears the wooded slopes of Anstiebury Camp, one of Surrey's finest Iron Age hillforts, dating from the second century BC; its ramparts enclose over 11 acres.

◄ Coldharbour
The Village c1955 C137012

This small and picturesque village lies on the east slopes of Leith Hill, the southern edge of the greensand ridge which climbs to 965 feet (295 metres) half a mile west of the village. Leith Hill is the highest point in Surrey, and it is raised to over 1000 feet by a tower that dates from 1765. This view looks north-east past Post Box House on the right. On the left, beyond the three gables of Forge Cottage, is the former school, now converted to houses.

▼ Beare Green
The Duke's Head c1955
B41006

Back on the A24 London to Worthing Road, and north of Capel, is Beare Green with the Duke's Head pub. This now sits at the east side of a large roundabout of at least an acre, sited where the A24 and A29 London to Bognor roads diverge. The pub itself is little changed, except that the old outside gents' lavatory on its right has been replaced by brick lean-to lavatories accessed from within the pub.

◄ Beare Green
The Duke's Head
the Saloon Bar c1955 B41012

This splendid interior captures the atmosphere of a 1950s pub beautifully. The shirt-sleeved landlord, his hair slicked with Brylcreem, has his sleeves rolled up and a tie at his neck. The G-Plan style floral fabric-cushioned chairs, the odd stools, the horse brasses and the vertical timber boarded bar front are a wonderful evocation. Note the advertisement for 'Hot Bangers' above the bar: remember that fifty years ago, pub and food were words that did not go together, so this was an enterprising landlord.

◀ **Dorking
High Street c1955** D45049
Dorking's High Street is a
most attractive one, but
nowadays it is considerably
more traffic-choked than it
was in the 1950s. A good
piece of townscape, the street
both winds and undulates;
there are many good
buildings, such as the White
Horse Hotel on the right.
Woolworth's was rebuilt not
long after this view was taken;
in the process Richard Hicks
shop next door was
demolished, and all was
replaced by a pallid neo-
Georgian two-storey building.

◄ North Holmwood
Church Walk c1955 N41023

Now merged with Dorking, North Holmwood is one of three small villages along the west side of the large and mostly wooded Holmwood Common - the other two villages are Mid Holmwood and South Holmwood. Once the haunt of highwaymen, the common was given to the National Trust by the Duke of Norfolk in 1956. The Cabin is now part of the Forbuoys chain, but it is still the same sort of shop.

▼ Ranmore Common
The Post Office c1955 R358007

West of Dorking up on the chalk and just inboard of the North Downs escarpment, and west of the valley cut by the River Mole, is Ranmore Common. The village is scattered along the margins of a long green, and Frith's photographer took his near-obligatory post office view on the north side of the green. The house is L-shaped, and it is no longer either a post office or a tea room. The telephone box has gone too. The house is now called, unsurprisingly, The Old Post Office.

◄ Dorking
Box Hill, The Wimpy Bar c1965 D45205

When I was a teenager I remember riding out on my BSA Bantam to the Wimpy Bar on Box Hill. I seem to recall that we thought beefburgers and thick milk shakes the height of sophistication and 'cool'. Note the gimcrack structure with its fake pediments, and the waitress in white slip-ons, apron and bouffant hair - she may well have served me and my friends. The Wimpy Bar has long been replaced now.

Dorking
Box Hill, The Tea Gardens c1955 D45042

The tea gardens at the top of Box Hill were more genteel than the Wimpy Bar. The National Trust, who at first acquired 230 acres here in 1914, now own over 1200 acres of Box Hill, and the tea gardens are no more. This late 19th-century building survives behind a new frontage. It is now National Trust tea rooms, restaurant and servery, while other blocks have been built to the left for the Trust's shop and an information centre, linked to it by walls. The views from here towards the Weald are superb.

Brockham, The Royal Oak c1965 B224054

This very attractive village has a fine triangular green dominated on the south side by its remarkably apt parish church, which from a distance looks as though it has always been there. In fact, it only dates from 1846. Brockham became a parish soon after, in 1848, when it was separated from nearby Betchworth. The green is used for cricket, as it has been since at least the 18th century; in the 19th century W G Grace played here.

Brockham, The Green c1965 B224013

This view, taken from the start of Tanner's Hill, looks north-east across the green and past the parish pump in its tiled pumphouse to the Royal Oak pub and a fine range of historic houses and cottages. Ashdown's shop is now a house named Ashdown Cottage. To the left of the Royal Oak, the small cottage with two dormers is called Thimble Cottage.

▼ **Brockham, Old School Lane c1955** B224019

Further down Tanner's Hill, the lane becomes Old School Lane; this view looks north past these pairs of tile-hung former estate cottages, which are all now in private hands and extended by a bay at each end. Beyond is Pondtail Farm, a part 16th- and 17th-century farmhouse, again with tile-hanging, and with early brick chimneys. Beyond is the escarpment of the North Downs at Box Hill.

▼ **Buckland, Post Office Corner c1955** B596018

This small village is situated on the A25 Dorking to Reigate road, and is cut in two by heavy traffic. To the north is a pretty pond, and to the south of the main road is the excellent dark brown greensand sandstone parish church, rebuilt apart from the belfry timber posts in 1860. In the foreground, on the corner of Dungates Lane, is this 16th-century timber-framed house, now subdivided; its left gabled crosswing is a house, and the rest is now the Buckland Stores, and all virtually unchanged.

▲ **Headley**
The Cock c1955 H61003

Moving north, the route climbs onto the North Downs to Headley and the Cock pub, now called the Cock Horse. This view looks from the garden of the Old School House, built in about 1850, and once the village school, of course. Out of sight, screened by trees, is the parish churchyard and the Victorian church; to the south of the church stands the old font in a niche below a 13th-century arch from the old church.

◄ **Leatherhead
High Street c1955** L26007
Leatherhead is, like Dorking, a town on the River Mole, but it has suffered much architectural loss in recent years. Attempts to make amends include pedestrianising the High Street, but many of the buildings seen in this view, particularly on the left-hand side, have gone, including the 1880s Barclays Bank, which is now a building at the entrance to the 1980s Swan Shopping Centre. Further along, also on the left, is Cradle's House, a 14th-century hall house, which has recently been restored, a sad reminder of what the town has lost.

Leatherhead
Bridge Street c1955 L26044

We are looking up Bridge Street past the North Street junction. The streetscape is dominated by the former Burton's building, an urban interloper of 1939 with its giant Ionic pilasters supporting a heavy cornice. This is something of a contrast to the mock-Tudor bank with its three storeys of timber-framing, now the Woolwich. Further downhill and behind the cameraman is the Running Horse pub, an important 14th-century building, and then the bridge over the Mole.

Little Bookham, Little Bookham Street c1955 L55002
The Bookhams and Fetcham retain old cores amid the great suburban expansion which occurred after World War II; they are in effect western suburbs of Leatherhead across the River Mole. Little Bookham's tiny 12th-century church and manor house lie south of the Guildford Road. North of this east-west road, Little Bookham Street has some older buildings amid the suburbia and wide grassy verges. This view looks across to the general store and post office; its clock, inscribed 'Weale's Coal Order Office', and Howard Weale's shop sign both survive. In the distance there is a green London Transport country bus.

Great Bookham, High Street c1955 G51034
This view looks south. The High Street runs from the parish church, with its white-painted weatherboarded tower, to the Guildford road in the distance. The whitewashed Royal Oak (right) has a recessed centre to provide a small forecourt for benches; beyond is No 24, a good Georgian house with a mansard roof. On the left the builder Brackenbury and Sons replaced its sheds by a 1960s building of little merit, but at least the firm is still in the village.

▼ **Effingham, St Teresa's Convent c1965** E26048
St Teresa's Convent was established in Effinghamhill House, a stucco early 19th-century mansion in the chalk hills two miles south of Effingham village. Frith's photographer has caught a wonderful moment: a monk with his dark glasses and cigarette basks in the sunshine, with his dog idling too. Back in the village, opposite the Effingham Golf Club (whose club house is another stucco 19th-century house, Effingham House), is St Teresa's Preparatory School; it occupies Grove House, an elegant yellow stock brick house of about 1820.

▼ **East Horsley, Guildford Lodge c1965** H120105
A mile or so west of Effingham, the Guildford road cranks past a medieval fairy-tale castle. These twin towers with conical roofs flank a gateway that now only leads to a 20th-century housing estate, but it once led to The Towers, which we can see in view H120058. Dating from about 1860, the gatehouse is a fantastical construction of flintwork walling with a welter of brick enrichment. It seems to have dropped in from the Rhineland - a most unexpected style in the heart of Surrey.

▲ **East Horsley
The Towers c1955**
H120058
The estate was inherited by the Earl of Lovelace in the 1830s. The Earl was the son-in-law of Lord Byron, and he indulged his architectural tastes to the hilt, only getting fully into the swing of it after travels in Germany in the 1850s. This view shows the Rhineland-style tower he added in 1858 - he added much more besides. Currently a management college, and private property, entry is via a gate-house further up Ockham Road South, not via the Guildford Lodge (H120105).

◀ **East Clandon
The Village c1955** E175011
This village was once known as Clandon Abbots, for its manor, as in many other Surrey villages, was owned by the local abbey. Here, Chertsey Abbey owned the manor from about 666 AD. The parish church behind the holly hedge to the left at the corner of Ripley Road is partly Norman. The village has many attractive timber-framed and brick houses and cottages, now kept in immaculate order; these include Bay Tree Cottage on the left and Church Cottage on the right, which has exposed 17th-century timber framing.

◄ Abinger Common
Wotton House, the Hunt c1965
A17032

The diarist John Evelyn described the 'delicious streames and venerable Woods' around Wotton. He was born in Wotton House in 1620 and inherited it later in the century; he died in 1706 and was buried in the fine parish church, which is isolated in the fields north of the A25. Some of the house he knew remains, but most of it is now Victorian, providing a backdrop for one of the Frith photographers' favourite themes: the hunt (not a theme likely to be a postcard best-seller today).

Abinger Hammer
The Village c1955 A18003

Across the chalk ridge, the route returns to the greensand country, and to one of Surrey's prettiest and most wooded areas. Abinger Hammer is most well known for its spectacular clock, which is attached to the corner of a typical late 19th-century Surrey vernacular tile-hung house. The house was tea-rooms in the 1950s, and still is today. The clock was rebuilt in 1891 for Lord Farrer of Abinger Hall: a blacksmith figure strikes the bell every hour. The village is somewhat traffic-choked - it is situated on the A25 - but the Abinger Arms beyond the clock also offers refreshment.

Holmbury St Mary
The Post Office c1965 H97052

The Frith photographer's desire to take views of post offices has led him to ignore the beautifully-situated village centre around its green and also the good 1879 church, designed, built and paid for by the architect George Edmund Street and surrounded by a backdrop of woods. Instead, he took his camera down Pitland Street to the south. This pair of 19th-century cottages with their bracket door hoods survive: the one on the right was the post office with a shop in the garden, which has now been demolished. The cottage is now named The Old Post Office.

Peaslake
The Village Green
c1955 P16009

Peaslake is a small village west of Holmbury St Mary, separated from it by a ridge of wooded hills. It lies along the slopes of a narrow valley at the head of a stream that flows towards the Tilling Bourne. This view, looking north to Peaslake Lane, is little changed, although the Forrest Stores is now the Peaslake Village Stores and thriving still.

◄ **Farley Green**
The Village c1955 F190004
Farley Green is situated towards the south end of Albury parish, and its fields are carved out of the surrounding greensand woods. The hamlet is centred upon a long hour-glass-shaped green; this view was taken at its north end, with Shophouse Lane on the right and August Lane on the left. The 1920s Elm Tree Cottage on the left is now partly hidden by a large beech tree, while the 19th-century cottages behind the pillar box (which is still there today) have an extra bay to the right.

◀ **Shere, The Village c1960** S114031

Shere, by-passed around the date this view was taken, was once a market town with a thriving fustian cloth industry; then it flourished thanks to watercress in the Tilling Bourne, which flows delightfully through the village. This view is taken from within the churchyard of St James's church, looking west into the Square with its elegant sandstone war memorial cross. The church is famous for its 13th-century anchoress or female hermit, Christine: she was the carpenter's daughter, and she was twice walled up in her cell against the wall of the church.

▼ **Blackheath, The Volunteer Arms c1955** B114015

To the west of Farley Heath and Blackheath, the hamlet of Blackheath grew up in Victorian times. The pub dates from about 1840, and used to have a later elaborate arched canopy, now long gone. The pub is now called the Villagers. The Watney's barrel over the sign is a period piece: remember Watney's Red Barrel beer? The lane leads onto Blackheath, which is popular with walkers.

◀ **Albury
The Village c1950** A25091

This chapter's tour finishes with an architectural flourish in Albury, a village still blighted by the A25. The main village was moved west and south of the Tilling Bourne and out of the park in the early 19th century, but the best buildings date from the 1850s. The medieval church and Albury Park are to the east and north of the stream, and are now on the North Downs Way long-distance footpath. These fine tile-hung houses are crowned by elaborate moulded brick Tudor-style chimneys. The Shell garage beyond has gone since the 1950s.

South-West Surrey

Farnham, The Borough c1955 F11038
Our fourth tour starts in one of Surrey's finest
towns, even if nowadays it is still traffic-blighted.
This view looks east along West Street to The
Borough, which starts beyond the white stucco
building (now gone) on the corner of Downing
Street. The Lion and Lamb Café on the left, a
close-studded timber-framed building built in
1537, is now the frontispiece to the Lion and Lamb
Yard shopping centre. Hedley Bartlett, the optician
on the right with the eye-catching sign, is now a
saddlery.

**Farnham
The Borough c1960**
F11071
The photographer is further east than he was when he took F11038, looking west along The Borough towards West Street. Just out of view to the right is Castle Street, Farnham's best street architecturally, with the Town Hall, a 1930s neo-Georgian building, on the Castle Street corner opposite the Queen's Head. The Brown Owl café is now the Sevens bar and restaurant. There is further continuity next door: Burtol the cleaners is now a Sketchleys branch, and Woolworth's still occupies its 1860s buildings.

Frensham, The Little Pond c1965 F47059

South of Farnham, on the greensand heathland, there are two famous and immensely popular lakes, Frensham Great Pond and Frensham Little Pond. The former was originally enlarged around 1200 to provide fish for the Bishop of Winchester's palace in Farnham. The Little Pond was dug in 1246, also as a 'stew' or fish pond for the Bishop. Nowadays the ponds are owned by the National Trust, along with Frensham Common with its pine woods and heaths, and they are still as much a major tourist attraction as they were in the 1960s.

Churt, The Crossways c1955 C105008

One of my earliest memories is of an early 1950s caravan holiday at Churt. Here, at about that time, Frith's photographer looks north along the main Hindhead-Farnham road towards the Crossways: this is what the main crossroads in Churt is called, and so is the pub at the right, a Courage house. Overton's Garage beyond the signpost has been rebuilt since, and is a smart Volvo garage now.

Churt
The Village c1965 C105021
We are a little further north than view C105008; we can see the BP
petrol pumps of Overton's Garage with the parade of shops beyond
the Crossways. The shop with the Hovis sign is the Crossways Churt
shop, which includes the village post office, while Phippards on the
right is still a newsagent and confectioner (now Churt News). Next
door, Smith's the chemists is now an Indian restaurant.

Hindhead, The Corner Shop c1965 H86056
This view looks east along the A3. While The Devil's Punchbowl, just east of Hindhead, is spectacularly beautiful, the central crossroads in Hindhead itself pictured in this view is utterly blighted by traffic. The A3 London to Portsmouth road crosses the Farnham to Chichester road here, and then, as now, the crossroads are traffic-light-controlled. The Corner Shop with its distinctive ogee-roofed corner turret has just been demolished (2001) for redevelopment.

Shottermill, The Village c1960 S124007
Although this view is titled Shottermill, strictly speaking it shows Springhead in Camelsdale just over the Hampshire border on the south bank of the young River Wey - Shottermill is on the north bank. This view looks along Camelsdale Road. The B2131 has been improved since 1960: there is a big roundabout now behind the camera, while the roads in the foreground and behind the war memorial have been removed and are now paths. The ponds were restored in 1955.

Haslemere
High Street c1955 H35004

Back in Surrey, the route reaches Haslemere; we look south-west along the High Street into the market place of this small town, with the 1814 Town Hall closing the vista. It is a spacious High Street, benefiting from the well-treed backdrop of the greensand hills beyond. On the right is the Georgian House Hotel in buildings dating from around 1740. The pavements are now more formalised, and the petrol pumps have gone from the left-hand side, although the building behind is still a car showroom.

◄ **Chiddingfold**
The Village c1955

C85005

This must be one of the most attractive villages in Surrey, with its large, sloping triangular green surrounded by good houses. The green is the scene of a spectacular bonfire on Guy Fawkes Night. This view is taken from the tower of St Mary's church on the other side of the A283, looking past the old forge with its heavily-pruned lime tree guardians.

◄ Grayswood, Grayswood Road c1955 G236010

Less than two miles north-east of Haslemere, Grayswood is a small parish carved out of Witley in 1900. It has a triangular village green out of view on the right, although the bell tower and spirelet of the church, completed in 1902, can be seen in the distance downhill. The houses (mostly of about 1890) remain, but several are almost hidden now by higher hedges. The village shop has gone, to be rebuilt as a two-storey house, Badgers Retreat.

▼ Chiddingfold, The Pond and the Village c1955
C85032

Back at ground level, this view looks across the pond near the church, past the railings alongside the A283 to the houses on the south side of the Green. The early 1950s bus shelter has now gone and no longer obscures the view. At the far right is the old forge, while Forrest Wine Stores has been replaced by a chemist's - Forrests have relocated to shops to the right of this view.

◄ Chiddingfold, Old Forge Cottage and the Village c1965 C85063

This attractive group, which makes the most of the possibilities of tile-hanging walls, is on the Petworth Road just south-west of the Green. The house on the left with its whitewashed tile-hangings is Old Forge Cottage, which apparently dates from 1321 - it was for sale at the time of the photograph. The two lime trees have now gone. Beyond, the shops have gone too, and the building is now Cyclops Cottage. The Swan pub is late Victorian, but it fits in well.

◀ **Dunsfold, The Post Office c1955** D68033
Dunsfold, north-west of Alfold, has a very large rectangular green, and the parish church of about 1270 is half a mile to the west. Frith's photographer has chosen to record the post office, a somewhat feeble piece of Surrey vernacular revival-style with a tile-hung first floor. The building still houses a shop, the Village Stores and Post Office, but the pillar box (in use in this view) has been moved to the right-hand side of the shop front.

◄ Alfold, The Village c1965
A302039

East of Chiddingfold the lanes wind to Alfold, which lies close to the Sussex border. This view looks south-west down Loxwood Road towards the parish church, whose spire can just be seen amid the trees behind the last chimney-stack. The houses in this view are for the most part late Victorian, apart from the one on the right; the prettiest part of the village is nearer the church and the Crown pub at the bottom of the hill.

▼ Hascombe, The Village c1965   H37002

Moving on north from Dunsfold, we come to Hascombe, a most attractive and tranquil village set in a curving wooded valley in the greensand hills. There is a large Iron Age hillfort at the end of Hascombe Hill's ridge a little south-east of the village. This view looks north along Godalming Road with the 18th-century White Horse pub on the right, its Bargate stone walls painted white. The cottage (Stable Cottage), the church of 1864 and most of the village houses not seen in this view are built in unpainted mellow golden Bargate stone.

◄ Witley, The Village c1955
W120013

Witley, further west on the Milford to Petworth road, is in total contrast: its houses are timber-framed, often with the upper storeys tile-hung. The tiles are in typical Surrey tile shapes with triangular ends or fish-scale effects, as we see here in Steps Cottage and Church Steps Cottage on the left (the churchyard steps are on the far left). Across the main road is the White Hart pub, 15th-century with a 16th-century main chimney. Out of sight to the left is a good Victorian timber-framed range.

Brook, The Dog and Pheasant c1955 B230006
A little south-west of Witley, the route passes the tile-hung Dog and Pheasant pub on the A286 Haslemere Road; it stands opposite the village cricket ground with the 1923 village hall. The pub is virtually unchanged today except for the right-hand building, which now has leaded light windows, and the external staircase has been glazed in, doubtless for safety reasons. Of course, the cars parked outside are rather different now.

Milford, The Crossroads c1965 M76028
From Brook the route heads to Milford, formerly partially on the A3 London to Portsmouth road but now, mercifully, by-passed - but the traffic is still heavy. This view is taken on the Portsmouth Road, now the A3100, with Church Road, the A286 Midhurst and Chichester road, heading to the left of the painted brick shop on the corner, which is now an Alldays store. Lloyds bank has gone, and its premises are now called Bargate House, and the tall lime tree in the garden of Vine Court (left of centre) is no more.

Milford
Spreading Fertiliser c1955 M76058
This photograph is included partly to show how farming has
changed in the last half century. In 1955 Frith's photographer
could still find farm horses at work, but they were becoming
sufficiently uncommon to warrant a photograph. This scene near
Milford shows a fertiliser spreader being hauled by a single horse.

Godalming
High Street c1955
G23039
Continuing north-east along Portsmouth Road we reach Godalming, a market town since 1300, its centre now by-passed. These timber-framed buildings are fine examples. We see them from beside the 1814 stuccoed Market Hall, at the junction of the High Street (now improved by traffic calming) and Church Street. Numbers 99-103, with their three jettied storeys which tower over the gabled timber-framed house on the right, are now a children's wear shop.

Godalming, Bridge Street c1955 G23046
East along the High Street with its many good buildings, including ones with ornate 17th-century brickwork or Georgian facades, Bridge Street bears left to descend towards the bridge of 1783 over the River Wey. Architecturally it also descends from the heights of the High Street, except for the timber-framed building on the left half way down. Beyond is the Borough Hall of 1906, uninspiringly neo-Georgian.

Bramley, High Street c1955 B181004
Bramley stands about four miles south of Guildford on the Horsham Road; it is a long village with a busy crossroads with Station Road (there has been no railway since the 1960s). This view was taken just south of the crossroads, looking down the High Street; the two pubs on the right are the Jolly Farmers and the Wheatsheaf. In the distance there are Victorian buildings - the Bramley Dairy, left of centre, is now a house. At the far left is the high churchyard wall to Holy Trinity church, yet another Surrey medieval church largely replaced in Victorian times.

Farncombe
Farncombe Street c1955 F10017
Across the River Wey from Godalming is Farncombe, once a
hamlet but now in effect a suburb of the town. Its architectural
highlight is the Wyatt Almshouses of 1622 on the Guildford Road;
but our view is in Farncombe Street, looking west to the railway
level crossing. The gates are now lifting barriers, but the signal box
survives. Unfortunately, the left-hand side of the street has largely
been rebuilt in sad 1960s three-storey flats-over-shops style: no
match for the 1930s mock timber-framed parade opposite.

◄ **Puttenham, The Post Office
and the Church c1955** P122005
Across the A3, Puttenham village
lies just south of the narrow chalk
ridge of the Hog's Back. A
greensand village, it is slightly off
the beaten track and quiet: or at
least quiet west of the B3000
Puttenham Hill road, which links
the A31 and the A3. This view
looks along one of these quiet
lanes, The Street, towards the
parish church, with the walls to
Puttenham Priory's grounds on
the right: no real priory this, but a
good stucco mansion of 1762.
The post office and library is now
a shop, the Iron Bed Company,
and the telephone kiosk has gone.

◀ **Compton, The Village c1955** C146032
North-west of Godalming, Compton is famed for the Watts Gallery and Chapel, commemorating the Victorian painter George Frederick Watts. I first visited the village many years ago for its superb Norman parish church. This view, looking downhill, is now barely recognisable: the cottages by the telegraph pole were cleared for 1960s road widening. Ellis, the baker and grocer (left), is now an antique shop. Beyond the Harrow Inn, the pub on the right, stands the village hall; its foundation stone was laid by Mrs Watts, the artist's widow, in 1934.

▼ **Elstead, The Green c1965** E31057
Moving west from Godalming, the route passes through Elstead, a village with a medieval bridge over the River Wey and this triangular village green. This view is taken from Milford Road, with Farnham Road at the right curving past the former blacksmith's forge, which is now a cottage, The Old Forge. The chemist on the left is still a chemist, now the Elstead Pharmacy, and Challis' store is now a Spar. The oak was planted in 1897 for Queen Victoria's diamond jubilee; it still dominates the green with its seat around the base.

◀ **Tilford, The River c1955**
T49005
Tilford is situated where the south branch of the River Wey meets the main River Wey, each branch crossed by a medieval bridge. This is the bridge over the main Wey, built in dark brown greensand or Bargate stone with timber fence parapets. Across the bridge is the Post Office and Store, the building with the two gables, while between it and the bridge, just discernible, is a concrete World War II concrete pillbox. There is a large triangular village green behind the photographer.

Guildford & West Surrey

Guildford, High Street c1955 G65002
The last chapter's tour starts in Guildford, a
cathedral city since 1927. Sir Edwin Maufe's
dignified and apt cathedral was only completed
in 1966, with much of the work dating from the
period spanned by this book. The town has a
superb situation on the chalk ridge, with a castle
south of the High Street; the ridge is cut through
by the River Wey. Many superb buildings
complement the townscape, and this 1950s view
looking west just before the major descent to the
river valley captures some of this quality. Note
the road with its stone setts rather than tarmac.

Guildford, The Roof Garden c1960 G65128

This view captures well the design ethos of the period. This roof garden was placed on top of Harvey's, a five-storey department store of 1957 designed by Jellicoe and Partners and built behind a retained High Street frontage. The garden survives, with its views over surrounding townscape and countryside. Harvey's is now House of Fraser with a large modern addition fronting North Street, and the restaurant is now French and classier, but at least this archetypal 1950s-designed roof garden is intact.

Ripley, High Street c1955 R36038

North-east of Guildford and now by-passed by the A3, Ripley has a long wide High Street and was full of coaching inns in earlier days. In 1955, of course, the A3 still passed through the centre, but nowadays the traffic is still heavy, despite the by-pass. The trees have now gone, and the Cedar Hotel (left), one of the former coaching inns, is now the Cedar House Gallery; the Snack Bar Café (centre right) is a car dealer today.

Woking
Chertsey Road c1960 W122071
Woking should not be confused with Old Woking a mile south on
the banks of the River Wey, a battered remnant of a medieval
market town. This Woking grew up when the railway arrived in
1838, and is now one of Surrey's biggest towns. This view looks
north-east along Chertsey Road (now one-way and traffic-calmed)
away from the station, which fuelled the commuter-based growth
of the town. Barclays Bank on the right is now Alldays
convenience store, and the distant view is now dominated
by tall 1990s offices, Dukes Court.

▼ **Chobham, High Street c1955** C395008

As we head north-west, we should find Chobham village to be a relief after the rather drear urban townscape of Woking; but the traffic levels in Chobham prevent a true village atmosphere prevailing. That said, it has some fine streetscapes, particularly around the church. This view looks along the High Street from the Vicarage Road junction, now a mini-roundabout. The Ascot District Gas & Electricity Company and Herbert's are no more: the building is now merged as Eden House and offices.

▼ **Chobham, High Street c1955** C395012

Standing opposite the start of the churchyard, Frith's photographer looks back along the High Street to the Vicarage Road junction and the A319 main Bagshot to Chertsey road. The White Hart has had the paint removed from its front and is now no longer a straightforward village pub, but a Bluebecker's Eating House. Beyond the shop is now Lloyds Pharmacy, whose good early 19th-century shopfront with fluted Doric columns is still intact.

▲ **Bagshot, High Street c1955** B4035

Frith's photographer has chosen the best bit of Bagshot to photograph: he is looking south-west along the High Street from its junction with Bridge Road towards the Square. The bridge in question crosses the Windle Brook. On the left is the Three Mariners pub, an 18th-century building, but standing beyond it now are overscaled two-storey offices. This quieter and more characterful part of Bagshot is by-passed by the London Road, and the M3 is not far away. To the north are the sandy heaths on the geological strata known as Bagshot Sands.

◄ **Camberley, London Road c1955** C12019
Camberley lies on the south side of the A30. On the north side are the grounds of the Royal Military Academy, Sandhurst, which are mostly in Berkshire; but its Greek Doric gate lodges front London Road. On the Camberley side the Municipal Building of 1906, now converted to flats, is all that survives of this view now. The building on the far right has gone, as have all those to the left, the latter replaced by appalling pastiche developer neo-Georgian flats, proudly dated 2001. Behind the conifer is now the Council's Arena Leisure Centre.

**Camberley
High Street c1955**

C12028

We are looking south down the High Street, which runs from London Road towards the railway station. Crawley Hill is in the distance, covered in more spacious suburbs. Much in the middle distance has been rebuilt, but most of the nearer buildings survive. An exception is the single-storey shops on the right, which have been replaced by a nasty three-storey flat-roofed 1960s building. Out of view to the right is the very large Main Square Shopping Centre with its Noddy in Toyland-style porticoes.

◀ **Frimley Green
The Green c1965** F51035
About a mile south, along the
B3411, is Frimley Green. Frith's
photographer is looking from
the middle of the green
towards Wharf Road, with the
through road crossing the
centre of the view. The junction
now has a mini-roundabout,
which is very necessary in this
traffic-choked area: try crossing
the road to the green. The
uninspiring shops and flats on
the left were built around
1960, while the shop on the
right, a late Victorian building
with mock timber-framing, is
now empty (October 2001).

◀ **Frimley, Frimley Street c1955** F50054
Frimley is nowadays separated from
Camberley by the M3 and a complex of
roundabouts and dual carriageways; it
has expanded greatly since 1955.
Discerning the pattern of the village is
now difficult, but originally it grew up
east of the Blackwater River, the county
boundary. This view looks east along
the High Street away from the railway
station towards one of the older
buildings, Ye Olde Whyte Hart, now
beyond a big roundabout. On the left is
the Radway Arms, which still survives,
but much else has been rebuilt in the
1960s, particularly on the right.

▼ **Bisley, The Hen and Chickens
c1955** B109004
East of Camberley, the route moves
on to the villages between Bagshot
and Guildford along the A322 on
the east side of the sandy heathland
of the Bagshot Sands; on the map
we see army firing ranges marked
'Danger Area'. This is one of the
pubs along the A322 at the south
end of Bisley's village green. The
Hen and Chickens, now a Courage
house, has a 17th-century timber-
framed central section, and all the
elevations are now white-painted.
The sheds and outside toilets on the
left have been rebuilt, and the fir
tree has gone.

◀ **Bisley
The Century Range
c1955** B109022
This view is of the
famous National Rifle
Association target-
shooting range at Bisley,
where the annual world
championship shooting
competitions are held.
The ranges run south-
east to north-west, with
the targets below the
number boards on the
bund, or earthwork,
behind them.

Brookwood, The Basingstoke Canal c1955 B232014
This photograph was taken from Pirbright Bridge, where Queens Road leaves the A324 and leads to Pirbright Barracks and the Bisley rifle ranges. The Basingstoke Canal, opened in 1794, was in decay in the 1950s, but it has been restored to reopen in 1991. This view is of Pirbright Lock, No 15; we are looking past the lock keeper's cottage (then a café, now a private house) to the girder bridge across the canal. This carried a railway serving Pirbright and Bisley Army Camps, but it is no more: only the left-hand pier of the bridge remains.

Pirbright, The Pond c1960 P54002
The last view in this chapter and in the book looks from the large village green across the pond to housing typical of the development of Pirbright. The green was heathland, and the village basically dates from the mid 19th century, although there are a few older buildings, such as the Cricketers pub at the far left. Little has changed here. Many cottages carry plaques with the 'P' of Lord Pirbright, the village developer and estate owner. The trees, the bench and the post office remain.

Index

Frith Book Co Titles

www.francisfrith.co.uk

The Frith Book Company publishes over 100 new titles each year. A selection of those currently available are listed below. For latest catalogue please contact Frith Book Co.

Town Books 96 pages, approx 100 photos. County and Themed Books 128 pages, approx 150 photos (unless specified). All titles hardback laminated case and jacket except those indicated pb (paperback)

Title	ISBN	Price
Amersham, Chesham & Rickmansworth (pb)	1-85937-340-2	£9.99
Ancient Monuments & Stone Circles	1-85937-143-4	£17.99
Aylesbury (pb)	1-85937-227-9	£9.99
Bakewell	1-85937-113-2	£12.99
Barnstaple (pb)	1-85937-300-3	£9.99
Bath (pb)	1-85937419-0	£9.99
Bedford (pb)	1-85937-205-8	£9.99
Berkshire (pb)	1-85937-191-4	£9.99
Berkshire Churches	1-85937-170-1	£17.99
Blackpool (pb)	1-85937-382-8	£9.99
Bognor Regis (pb)	1-85937-431-x	£9.99
Bournemouth	1-85937-067-5	£12.99
Bradford (pb)	1-85937-204-x	£9.99
Brighton & Hove(pb)	1-85937-192-2	£8.99
Bristol (pb)	1-85937-264-3	£9.99
British Life A Century Ago (pb)	1-85937-213-9	£9.99
Buckinghamshire (pb)	1-85937-200-7	£9.99
Camberley (pb)	1-85937-222-8	£9.99
Cambridge (pb)	1-85937-422-0	£9.99
Cambridgeshire (pb)	1-85937-420-4	£9.99
Canals & Waterways (pb)	1-85937-291-0	£9.99
Canterbury Cathedral (pb)	1-85937-179-5	£9.99
Cardiff (pb)	1-85937-093-4	£9.99
Carmarthenshire	1-85937-216-3	£14.99
Chelmsford (pb)	1-85937-310-0	£9.99
Cheltenham (pb)	1-85937-095-0	£9.99
Cheshire (pb)	1-85937-271-6	£9.99
Chester	1-85937-090-x	£12.99
Chesterfield	1-85937-378-x	£9.99
Chichester (pb)	1-85937-228-7	£9.99
Colchester (pb)	1-85937-188-4	£8.99
Cornish Coast	1-85937-163-9	£14.99
Cornwall (pb)	1-85937-229-5	£9.99
Cornwall Living Memories	1-85937-248-1	£14.99
Cotswolds (pb)	1-85937-230-9	£9.99
Cotswolds Living Memories	1-85937-255-4	£14.99
County Durham	1-85937-123-x	£14.99
Croydon Living Memories	1-85937-162-0	£9.99
Cumbria	1-85937-101-9	£14.99
Dartmoor	1-85937-145-0	£14.99
Derby (pb)	1-85937-367-4	£9.99
Derbyshire (pb)	1-85937-196-5	£9.99
Devon (pb)	1-85937-297-x	£9.99
Dorset (pb)	1-85937-269-4	£9.99
Dorset Churches	1-85937-172-8	£17.99
Dorset Coast (pb)	1-85937-299-6	£9.99
Dorset Living Memories	1-85937-210-4	£14.99
Down the Severn	1-85937-118-3	£14.99
Down the Thames (pb)	1-85937-278-3	£9.99
Down the Trent	1-85937-311-9	£14.99
Dublin (pb)	1-85937-231-7	£9.99
East Anglia (pb)	1-85937-265-1	£9.99
East London	1-85937-080-2	£14.99
East Sussex	1-85937-130-2	£14.99
Eastbourne	1-85937-061-6	£12.99
Edinburgh (pb)	1-85937-193-0	£8.99
England in the 1880s	1-85937-331-3	£17.99
English Castles (pb)	1-85937-434-4	£9.99
English Country Houses	1-85937-161-2	£17.99
Essex (pb)	1-85937-270-8	£9.99
Exeter	1-85937-126-4	£12.99
Exmoor	1-85937-132-9	£14.99
Falmouth	1-85937-066-7	£12.99
Folkestone (pb)	1-85937-124-8	£9.99
Glasgow (pb)	1-85937-190-6	£9.99
Gloucestershire	1-85937-102-7	£14.99
Great Yarmouth (pb)	1-85937-426-3	£9.99
Greater Manchester (pb)	1-85937-266-x	£9.99
Guildford (pb)	1-85937-410-7	£9.99
Hampshire (pb)	1-85937-279-1	£9.99
Hampshire Churches (pb)	1-85937-207-4	£9.99
Harrogate	1-85937-423-9	£9.99
Hastings & Bexhill (pb)	1-85937-131-0	£9.99
Heart of Lancashire (pb)	1-85937-197-3	£9.99
Helston (pb)	1-85937-214-7	£9.99
Hereford (pb)	1-85937-175-2	£9.99
Herefordshire	1-85937-174-4	£14.99
Hertfordshire (pb)	1-85937-247-3	£9.99
Horsham (pb)	1-85937-432-8	£9.99
Humberside	1-85937-215-5	£14.99
Hythe, Romney Marsh & Ashford	1-85937-256-2	£9.99

Available from your local bookshop or from the publisher

Frith Book Co Titles (continued)

Title	ISBN	Price	Title	ISBN	Price
Ipswich (pb)	1-85937-424-7	£9.99	St Ives (pb)	1-85937415-8	£9.99
Ireland (pb)	1-85937-181-7	£9.99	Scotland (pb)	1-85937-182-5	£9.99
Isle of Man (pb)	1-85937-268-6	£9.99	Scottish Castles (pb)	1-85937-323-2	£9.99
Isles of Scilly	1-85937-136-1	£14.99	Sevenoaks & Tunbridge	1-85937-057-8	£12.99
Isle of Wight (pb)	1-85937-429-8	£9.99	Sheffield, South Yorks (pb)	1-85937-267-8	£9.99
Isle of Wight Living Memories	1-85937-304-6	£14.99	Shrewsbury (pb)	1-85937-325-9	£9.99
Kent (pb)	1-85937-189-2	£9.99	Shropshire (pb)	1-85937-326-7	£9.99
Kent Living Memories	1-85937-125-6	£14.99	Somerset	1-85937-153-1	£14.99
Lake District (pb)	1-85937-275-9	£9.99	South Devon Coast	1-85937-107-8	£14.99
Lancaster, Morecambe & Heysham (pb)	1-85937-233-3	£9.99	South Devon Living Memories	1-85937-168-x	£14.99
Leeds (pb)	1-85937-202-3	£9.99	South Hams	1-85937-220-1	£14.99
Leicester	1-85937-073-x	£12.99	Southampton (pb)	1-85937-427-1	£9.99
Leicestershire (pb)	1-85937-185-x	£9.99	Southport (pb)	1-85937-425-5	£9.99
Lincolnshire (pb)	1-85937-433-6	£9.99	Staffordshire	1-85937-047-0	£12.99
Liverpool & Merseyside (pb)	1-85937-234-1	£9.99	Stratford upon Avon	1-85937-098-5	£12.99
London (pb)	1-85937-183-3	£9.99	Suffolk (pb)	1-85937-221-x	£9.99
Ludlow (pb)	1-85937-176-0	£9.99	Suffolk Coast	1-85937-259-7	£14.99
Luton (pb)	1-85937-235-x	£9.99	Surrey (pb)	1-85937-240-6	£9.99
Maidstone	1-85937-056-x	£14.99	Sussex (pb)	1-85937-184-1	£9.99
Manchester (pb)	1-85937-198-1	£9.99	Swansea (pb)	1-85937-167-1	£9.99
Middlesex	1-85937-158-2	£14.99	Tees Valley & Cleveland	1-85937-211-2	£14.99
New Forest	1-85937-128-0	£14.99	Thanet (pb)	1-85937-116-7	£9.99
Newark (pb)	1-85937-366-6	£9.99	Tiverton (pb)	1-85937-178-7	£9.99
Newport, Wales (pb)	1-85937-258-9	£9.99	Torbay	1-85937-063-2	£12.99
Newquay (pb)	1-85937-421-2	£9.99	Truro	1-85937-147-7	£12.99
Norfolk (pb)	1-85937-195-7	£9.99	Victorian and Edwardian Cornwall	1-85937-252-x	£14.99
Norfolk Living Memories	1-85937-217-1	£14.99	Victorian & Edwardian Devon	1-85937-253-8	£14.99
Northamptonshire	1-85937-150-7	£14.99	Victorian & Edwardian Kent	1-85937-149-3	£14.99
Northumberland Tyne & Wear (pb)	1-85937-281-3	£9.99	Vic & Ed Maritime Album	1-85937-144-2	£17.99
North Devon Coast	1-85937-146-9	£14.99	Victorian and Edwardian Sussex	1-85937-157-4	£14.99
North Devon Living Memories	1-85937-261-9	£14.99	Victorian & Edwardian Yorkshire	1-85937-154-x	£14.99
North London	1-85937-206-6	£14.99	Victorian Seaside	1-85937-159-0	£17.99
North Wales (pb)	1-85937-298-8	£9.99	Villages of Devon (pb)	1-85937-293-7	£9.99
North Yorkshire (pb)	1-85937-236-8	£9.99	Villages of Kent (pb)	1-85937-294-5	£9.99
Norwich (pb)	1-85937-194-9	£8.99	Villages of Sussex (pb)	1-85937-295-3	£9.99
Nottingham (pb)	1-85937-324-0	£9.99	Warwickshire (pb)	1-85937-203-1	£9.99
Nottinghamshire (pb)	1-85937-187-6	£9.99	Welsh Castles (pb)	1-85937-322-4	£9.99
Oxford (pb)	1-85937-411-5	£9.99	West Midlands (pb)	1-85937-289-9	£9.99
Oxfordshire (pb)	1-85937-430-1	£9.99	West Sussex	1-85937-148-5	£14.99
Peak District (pb)	1-85937-280-5	£9.99	West Yorkshire (pb)	1-85937-201-5	£9.99
Penzance	1-85937-069-1	£12.99	Weymouth (pb)	1-85937-209-0	£9.99
Peterborough (pb)	1-85937-219-8	£9.99	Wiltshire (pb)	1-85937-277-5	£9.99
Piers	1-85937-237-6	£17.99	Wiltshire Churches (pb)	1-85937-171-x	£9.99
Plymouth	1-85937-119-1	£12.99	Wiltshire Living Memories	1-85937-245-7	£14.99
Poole & Sandbanks (pb)	1-85937-251-1	£9.99	Winchester (pb)	1-85937-428-x	£9.99
Preston (pb)	1-85937-212-0	£9.99	Windmills & Watermills	1-85937-242-2	£17.99
Reading (pb)	1-85937-238-4	£9.99	Worcester (pb)	1-85937-165-5	£9.99
Romford (pb)	1-85937-319-4	£9.99	Worcestershire	1-85937-152-3	£14.99
Salisbury (pb)	1-85937-239-2	£9.99	York (pb)	1-85937-199-x	£9.99
Scarborough (pb)	1-85937-379-8	£9.99	Yorkshire (pb)	1-85937-186-8	£9.99
St Albans (pb)	1-85937-341-0	£9.99	Yorkshire Living Memories	1-85937-166-3	£14.99

See Frith books on the internet www.francisfrith.co.uk

FRITH PRODUCTS & SERVICES

Francis Frith would doubtless be pleased to know that the pioneering publishing venture he started in 1860 still continues today. A hundred and forty years later, The Francis Frith Collection continues in the same innovative tradition and is now one of the foremost publishers of vintage photographs in the world. Some of the current activities include:

Interior Decoration

Today Frith's photographs can be seen framed and as giant wall murals in thousands of pubs, restaurants, hotels, banks, retail stores and other public buildings throughout the country. In every case they enhance the unique local atmosphere of the places they depict and provide reminders of gentler days in an increasingly busy and frenetic world.

Product Promotions

Frith products are used by many major companies to promote the sales of their own products or to reinforce their own history and heritage. Frith promotions have been used by Hovis bread, Courage beers, Scots Porage Oats, Colman's mustard, Cadbury's foods, Mellow Birds coffee, Dunhill pipe tobacco, Guinness, and Bulmer's Cider.

Genealogy and Family History

As the interest in family history and roots grows world-wide, more and more people are turning to Frith's photographs of Great Britain for images of the towns, villages and streets where their ancestors lived; and, of course, photographs of the churches and chapels where their ancestors were christened, married and buried are an essential part of every genealogy tree and family album.

Frith Products

All Frith photographs are available Framed or just as Mounted Prints and Posters (size 23 x 16 inches). These may be ordered from the address below. From time to time other products - Address Books, Calendars, Table Mats, etc - are available.

The Internet

Already twenty thousand Frith photographs can be viewed and purchased on the internet through the Frith websites and a myriad of partner sites.

For more detailed information on Frith companies and products, look at these sites:

www.francisfrith.co.uk
www.francisfrith.com
(for North American visitors)

See the complete list of Frith Books at:

www.francisfrith.co.uk

This web site is regularly updated with the latest list of publications from the Frith Book Company. If you wish to buy books relating to another part of the country that your local bookshop does not stock, you may purchase on-line.

For further information, trade, or author enquiries please contact us at the address below:
The Francis Frith Collection, Frith's Barn, Teffont, Salisbury, Wiltshire, England SP3 5QP.
Tel: +44 (0)1722 716 376 Fax: +44 (0)1722 716 881   Email: sales@francisfrith.co.uk

See Frith books on the internet www.francisfrith.co.uk

TO RECEIVE YOUR FREE MOUNTED PRINT

Mounted Print
Overall size 14 x 11 inches

Cut out this Voucher and return it with your remittance for £1.95 to cover postage and handling, to UK addresses. For overseas addresses please include £4.00 post and handling. Choose any photograph included in this book. Your SEPIA print will be A4 in size, and mounted in a cream mount with burgundy rule line, overall size 14 x 11 inches.

Order additional Mounted Prints at HALF PRICE (only £7.49 each*)

If there are further pictures you would like to order, possibly as gifts for friends and family, purchase them at half price (no additional postage and handling required).

Have your Mounted Prints framed*

For an additional £14.95 per print you can have your chosen Mounted Print framed in an elegant polished wood and gilt moulding, overall size 16 x 13 inches (no additional postage and handling required).

---

* IMPORTANT!
These special prices are only available if ordered using the original voucher on this page (no copies permitted) and at the same time as your free Mounted Print, for delivery to the same address

---

Frith Collectors' Guild

From time to time we publish a magazine of news and stories about Frith photographs and further special offers of Frith products. If you would like 12 months FREE membership, please return this form.

Send completed forms to:
The Francis Frith Collection, Frith's Barn, Teffont, Salisbury, Wiltshire SP3 5QP

Voucher for FREE and Reduced Price Frith Prints

Picture no.	Page number	Qty	Mounted @ £7.49	Framed + £14.95	Total Cost
		1	**Free of charge***	£	£
			£7.49	£	£
			£7.49	£	£
			£7.49	£	£
			£7.49	£	£
			£7.49	£	£

Please allow 28 days for delivery	*** Post & handling**	£1.95
Book Title	**Total Order Cost**	£

Please do not photocopy this voucher. Only the original is valid, so please cut it out and return it to us.

I enclose a cheque / postal order for £ . . . .
made payable to 'The Francis Frith Collection'
OR please debit my Mastercard / Visa / Switch / Amex card
(credit cards please on all overseas orders)

Number . . . .

Issue No (Switch only) . . . . .Valid from (Amex/Switch) . . . .

Expires . . . . Signature . . . .

Name Mr/Mrs/Ms . . . .

Address . . . .

. . . .

. . . . Postcode . . . .

Daytime Tel No . . . .   Valid to 31/12/03

The Francis Frith Collectors' Guild

Please enrol me as a member for 12 months free of charge.

Name Mr/Mrs/Ms . . . .

Address . . . .

. . . .

. . . . Postcode . . . .

Would you like to find out more about Francis Frith?

We have recently recruited some entertaining speakers who are happy to visit local groups, clubs and societies to give an illustrated talk documenting Frith's travels and photographs. If you are a member of such a group and are interested in hosting a presentation, we would love to hear from you.

Our speakers bring with them a small selection of our local town and county books, together with sample prints. They are happy to take orders. A small proportion of the order value is donated to the group who have hosted the presentation. The talks are therefore an excellent way of fundraising for small groups and societies.

Can you help us with information about any of the Frith photographs in this book?

We are gradually compiling an historical record for each of the photographs in the Frith archive. It is always fascinating to find out the names of the people shown in the pictures, as well as insights into the shops, buildings and other features depicted.

If you recognize anyone in the photographs in this book, or if you have information not already included in the author's caption, do let us know. We would love to hear from you, and will try to publish it in future books or articles.

Our production team

Frith books are produced by a small dedicated team at offices in the converted Grade II listed 18th-century barn at Teffont near Salisbury, illustrated above. Most have worked with the Frith Collection for many years. All have in common one quality: they have a passion for the Frith Collection. The team is constantly expanding, but currently includes:

Jason Buck, John Buck, Douglas Burns, Heather Crisp, Lucy Elcock, Isobel Hall, Rob Hames, Hazel Heaton, Peter Horne, James Kinnear, Tina Leary, Hannah Marsh, Eliza Sackett, Terence Sackett, Sandra Sanger, Lewis Taylor, Shelley Tolcher, Helen Vimpany, Clive Wathen and Jenny Wathen.